BRITAIN IN OLD PHOTOGRAPHS

LANCING & SOMPTING

A SECOND SELECTION

PHILIP FRY

SUTTON PUBLISHING LIMITED

Sutton Publishing Limited
Phoenix Mill · Thrupp · Stroud
Gloucestershire · GL5 2BU

First published 1998

Photograph, page 1: Trevett's tobacco and
confectionery shop, Blenheim Terrace.

British Library Cataloguing in Publication Data
A catalogue record for this book is available from the
British Library.

ISBN 0-7509-1363-0

Typeset in 10/12 Perpetua.
Typesetting and origination by
Sutton Publishing Limited.
Printed in Great Britain by
Ebenezer Baylis, Worcester.

I would like to dedicate this book to all the people connected
with Lancing and Sompting who have helped me to achieve
the publication of my two books.

CONTENTS

INTRODUCTION

After the success of my first publication, *Lancing & Sompting in Old Photographs* (October 1995), I have been fortunate enough to be able to present this second book. It gives me an opportunity to cover areas of interest and importance that were omitted in my first book, owing to either lack of space or material. As the books are centred on old photographs, I felt it would be interesting to have a chapter devoted to the 'Golden Age' photographic family, the McCarthy brothers, who came to the village of South Lancing in 1908. William and Mary McCarthy had two daughters, Eileen and Gladys, and two sons, Norman and Eric. William was an artist and photographer, while Norman and Eric were photographers. My two books would not have been possible without them.

Since the publication of my first book a lot of extra information has come to light, including dates and names to faces. These are as follows: page 37: Black & White Minstrel Troupe, third from left at the back is Charlie White, third from the right is Dorothy Upfield; page 58: North Lancing Primary School, Billy Baker is next to George Kirk; page 71: Youth Club, Mary Power is next to Nancy Muggeridge and Joyce Avon should read Joyce Aburn; page 83: Bob Macguiness should read Bob McInnes; page 90: the date should be 1944.

If you have any information or photos that you feel are relevant to this book, or to the history of the villages of Lancing and Sompting, feel free to contact me through the publishers.

ACKNOWLEDGEMENTS

As with my first book, many people from both villages have contributed by lending photographs and giving information. My thanks go to the following: Derek, Cyril and Eddie Fry, Rita Dudley, the late Alex Page, Ken Matten, Christopher Passmore, Olive and Ted Webb, Peter Pescod, Mrs Tyas, Reg and Lily Wingfield, Doris Gammans, Emily Wood, Mrs Cox, Reg Picknell, P. Clements, Mike Prince, Peggy Barber, Bobby Squires, Doris Bailey, Winnie Paskin, Jack Chatfield, Len Green, Reg Bushby, George and Sheila Kirk, Don Marshall and Clive Nutter once again for his expertise in helping me cope with the computer!

Great care has been taken to ensure that no copyright has been violated. If this is the case, I apologise in advance: it was not intentional.

BIBLIOGRAPHY

Lancing and Sompting, Philip Fry
A History of Lancing, R.G.P. Kerridge
Kelly's Directories for Worthing & District
Around Old and New Shoreham, E. Colquhoun
A Short History of Shoreham Airport (pamphlet)

CHAPTER ONE

TRANSPORT

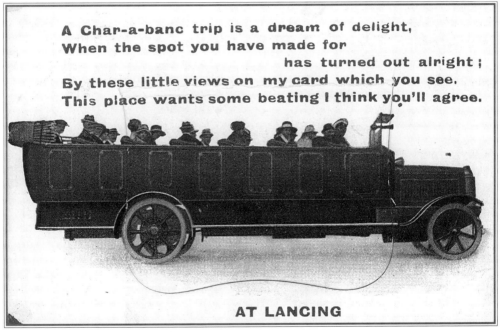

A Char-a-banc trip is a dream of delight,
When the spot you have made for
                    has turned out alright;
By these little views on my card which you see.
This place wants some beating I think you'll agree.

AT LANCING

Mailing novelty card, c. 1924. This particular type of card would have been mass produced and would have sold very well, as it was overprinted with the name of any town or village at the bottom of the card, the picture and rhyme staying the same. Inside there were twelve small views of the chosen locality, this one having views of Lancing. (Photochrom)

Continuing the theme of charabancs, here we see one waiting to set off from the Three Horse Shoes at South Lancing in the 1920s, when this form of outing was most popular. The gentleman third from the left in the waistcoat is George Prideaux jnr, who was the landlord from 1915 to 1931. He took over from his father, also George, who had the pub from 1878 to 1915. (McCarthy)

Eric Surfleet's Leyland double decker bus, *c.* 1964. It was a 1934 TD 3 chassis with a 1946 East Lancs body, and is seen here advertising the forthcoming Lancing Carnival organised by the Rotary Club. Eric was renowned for his fascination with buses, and had over 3,000 negatives of buses and coaches at his shop at 99 South Street, South Lancing. Transport photography was his business, which started in 1953 after he had spent twelve years as a bus conductor with Southdown Bus Company. (Surfleet)

Happy Days caravan site, *c.* 1953. The site was situated on the east side of Old Salts Farm Road, and at this time was relatively new. It was started up by a Maurice Bagel in 1947. At the entrance to the site was quite a grand display – a pond with water nymphs holding a bowl in the centre, and numerous urns and chimney pots full of blooms alongside various ornaments, which included a penguin, pelican, gnomes and a giant frog that sat in the pond! The site is now a mobile home park called Willowbrook.

Woolnough brothers' pick-up truck on the forecourt of their business, Lancing Motor Works, *c.* 1925. The garage was agent and distributor for Morris Cowley.

If you're going to have an accident, where better than outside your local garage! I would imagine this car was trying to turn left from South Street to get on to the Lower Brighton Road, and for some reason turned over. The gentleman with the bike seems totally unconcerned by it all and is looking elsewhere. This photograph dates from about 1926.

All manner of transport is seen here on the Lower Brighton Road. In the foreground is an F.W. Mitchell van, with the driver leaning against it with his delivery basket on his arm. The van came from Worthing to get more trade. With the coming of the motor vehicle it was easier and quicker for the companies to go farther afield. In the background a motorcycle and sidecar, a horse-drawn cart and horse-drawn wagon can be seen. The white-washed coastguard cottages and their fine flint wall are on the left. (Ward)

Potter Bailey & Co. horse and cart outside the granary up Mill Road, North Lancing. The address of High Street can be seen on the back of the cart: this was where their main shop at Worthing was located. Perhaps it was making a delivery to a customer on its way to the Lancing branch at South Street. (McCarthy)

A grand looking wagon, ready to set off on a procession from Lees Meadow, now Croshaw Rec, in 1919. This leads me to believe this was a peace parade to celebrate the end of the First World War. The children on the wagon are dressed in what looks like national dress of countries from the then British Empire. The route of the procession would most probably have taken in the manor grounds at North Lancing for a refreshments stop, then returned through the village back to Lees Meadow.

Bicycles were often decorated for processions, quite elaborately as can be seen here. These entrants were part of the peace parade mentioned in the previous caption. The lads in the top hats and black and white costumes were some of the Lancing Bonfire Boys. Many other associations would take part. These included Lancing coastguards, the Church Lads' Brigade, schoolchildren, the village brass band, members of the parish council, the Ancient Order of Foresters, Hearts of Oak societies and the Oddfellows, all of which I am sure made it a wonderful occasion!

Page & Stanbrook's wagon outside their baker's shop in Penhill Road, *c.* 1907. The business was established in 1904. Mr Stanbrook is holding the horse, Bob, with Mr Stanbrook's son sitting in the wagon with all the fresh bread waiting to be delivered. Even at this early date one of the company's specialities was doughnuts!

CHAPTER TWO

GROW YOUR OWN

Fruit picking, 1912, at one of Fuller's orchards, this one being in the area of Chester Avenue, South Lancing. 'In the shade of the old apple tree' was the apt title given to this photo by the photographer, McCarthy. At the top of the tree on the left is Martin Fuller; next to him, standing on the ladder, is Sid Fuller, a.k.a. Nidder. Left to right at the bottom are Edwin Fuller, Hector Boyd, Tom Boyd, Frank Fuller, a.k.a. Bloss, and Martin Fuller snr.

A nursery in South Lancing, September 1922. Stan Fuller, Leo Matten and Sid Fuller, who was the governor, are three of the men seen here, with what looks like a good crop of spuds! Note the Sussex trug sitting on the box, something nurserymen would not have been without at this time.

Mrs Prideaux, wife of landlord George snr, and her family outside the Three Horse Shoes pub, South Street, at the turn of the century. Landlords in this era would often find it hard to make ends meet on the sale of beer alone, so they would have other ways of earning extra income. George Prideaux had a nursery business situated to the south of Farmers Lane, now part of Kings Road. The cart was used to transport his produce.

Nursery at Alma Street, South Lancing, owned and run by Frederick Fuller, *c.* 1924. Shown here is what is known as a ¼ span greenhouse. The plants climbing up the wall are peaches. Below them in pots are arum lilies: as well as being saleable they also attracted insects into the greenhouse to pollinate the peaches. Another way to pollinate the peaches was to brush them with a rabbit's tail! (McCarthy)

Rosecroft Nursery, *c.* 1928. This nursery was owned by Frank Fuller, who lived in a house at the front of the nursery; the house was also known as Rosecroft, and was built in about 1922. Arthur Matten, who can be seen here behind the pile of mushroom compost, was the nursery foreman. The nursery and house are remembered by Rosecroft Close, which is near where the nursery was situated.

Tip-toeing through the tulips, 1922! These tulips and fruit trees were in the area we know as the Avenues, First, Second, etc. The land was owned at this time by D. Gooderham who lived at Newmans Farm, now known as Friars Acre in Manor Road, North Lancing. (McCarthy)

A fine show of daffodils, grown among the fruit trees, c. 1922. The rear of Malthouse Cottages, a.k.a. Grinstead Cottages, can be seen through the trees, which puts this scene in what is now Orchard Way. It looks very much a family affair with mum, dad and daughter, who would probably have been missing school to help with the gathering of the crop. (McCarthy)

The end of an era: Warren Nursery being sold at auction in 1964. The nursery was composed of 4¼ acres in Sompting Road, Lancing, next to the Warren Heart home for children (now Warren Court). The nursery was owned and run by Hartley and Woolgar. Like most nurseries its water was supplied from a borehole; the hole that supplied this nursery was 80 ft deep, and the water within was a constant temperature of 52 degrees in winter and summer!

The double wedding of Bessie and Dolly Bushby, c. 1912. The marriage between Bessie Bushby and Frank Fuller brought together two of the main produce growers in Lancing and Sompting. The wedding took place at St Mary's Church in Sompting. This photo was taken in the garden of Holmecroft, Cokeham Lane, home of Frank Bushby snr. Back row, left to right: -?-, Maggie Bushby, Ted Bushby. Middle row: Martin Fuller snr, Frank Fuller, Bessie Fuller (née Bushby), Dolly ? (née Bushby), Sid ?, Frank Bushby snr. Front row: Connie Luckin, Grace Snelling, -?-. Note Martin Fuller's 'friend' holding a basket of flowers. (McCarthy)

Staff of H. & A. Pullen-Burry Ltd, Sompting. In the middle of the nineteenth century John Pullen, who resided at Rectory House, West Street, started to build up a large market garden business, growing crops such as peaches, grapes, melons and vegetables. This was the forerunner to H. & A. Pullen-Burry Ltd, which was formed in 1931. Arthur Pullen-Burry also had land at South Lancing in the area of Old Salts Farm. At the start of the twentieth century the business had over 400 acres under cultivation.

Pullen-Burry staff posing for the camera with all their silverware for winning produce, behind Rectory House, West Street, Sompting, 1953. Standing, left to right: Fred Stringer, Ron Nye, Bert Cuckney, George Webly, Tom Meads, Fred Mills, Len Knight, Henry Etherington, George Izzard. Seated: Sid Fields, Maurice Nye, Charlie Goldsmith, ? Millyard, Frank Praill, Miss Viesy, Joe Barnes, Joe Burton.

CHAPTER THREE

BUSINESS

Page & Stanbrook, bakers, 1907. This shop was situated on the corner of Cecil Road and Penhill Road. As can be seen, deliveries were made at a slower pace than today, either by handcart or horse and cart. In 1909 Mr Stanbrook died, leaving his wife to take on his share of the business. Alex Page later bought the Stanbrook share of the business and the shop became the more familiar Page's bakery. They used to deliver to South and North Lancing, and into Worthing, this being where most trade was done. Alex Page in time sold out to F.W. Mitchell of Worthing.

A.G. Page's delivery horse and cart in 1910 posing for a photo in a Worthing street. This would have been near the end of the round, as their last call was in East Worthing before heading home to Lancing. The horse seen here went by the name of Bob, who liked nothing better than a swim in the sea at South Lancing! Freddy Nightingale is the driver, and the young man in the boater is Reg Page, brother to Alex.

The Lancing Motor Works, Lower Brighton Road, South Lancing. The opening of a major garage like this surely heralded the arrival of the motor car in the village. The works was owned by the Woolnough brothers, and opened in about 1925 when this photo was taken, perhaps to promote the works.

The interior of the workshop at the Lancing Motor Works, *c.* 1925. A lathe, drill, grinders and what look like tins of grease and oil on shelving are clearly prepared for any motor vehicle that has happened to break down.

Staff of the Three Horse Shoes pub taking a break to sample some ale, with two of Tamplin's draymen, the men in the leather aprons. The landlord, George Prideaux jnr, is at the rear looking over the crates; his brother Leo is standing next to him.

Potter Bailey & Co., grocers and provision merchants, 1910. The shop was situated on the corner of East Street and South Street, South Lancing, known locally as Potters Corner. The shop had an underground bakery, but in about 1900 this was condemned and closed down for health reasons. The shop opened in around 1897; the first manager was Ernest Rollings. It ceased trading in 1963, and was demolished in 1968. (McCarthy)

After Norman McCarthy departed from the family photographic business, Eric acquired this shop, using his middle name Justin as its title. Before this the shop had been a house, Chelmer House. The building was on the corner of South Street and East Street. Parts of the old garden wall can be seen here, adorned with plant urns, c. 1926. (McCarthy)

Martin George Fuller, a.k.a. Mart, had a fruiterer and greengrocer's shop in South Street. It would have been a natural progression for Mart to start up a shop as his father, also named Martin, had a market garden and nursery business, in South Lancing. Most of the goods for sale here would have been local and fresh. This photo pre-dates 1908 as Lovegrove Brothers' clothier's and outfitter's shop can be seen next door, and 1908 was the year in which they ceased trading.

Construction of a house in Cecil Road, South Lancing, 1903. These were the first homes in Lancing to have bathrooms built in! The scaffolding would have been in timber, most probably chestnut, and bound together by ropes. Being some time before cement mixers were thought of, the mix would have been knocked up in the large wooden tub, seen in the foreground, by hand. On the scaffold a plasterer's float is evident on a table, so one would assume they were in the process of rendering the face of the houses to give them a smooth finish.

No. 1 North Road, Lancing: E. Feldwick, grocer and provision dealer, 1906. This was a typical family-run village shop of the time, with Flo and Elizabeth Feldwick standing in the doorway and young Edward jnr standing next to his dad Edward Feldwick, holding his delivery basket. Note the interesting display of goods in the window. The Rowntree's cocoa advert spreads over three panes of glass: it shows how to make a cup of cocoa, from putting it in the cup to drinking the end product. Rowntree's proudly proclaimed that they were makers to the king!

Station Approach, North Road, 1929. This was just one of many small parades of shops that started to appear in the village to cope with the ever increasing population. Seen here are C.E.J. Burton, jeweller, J.A. Tonkyn, hairdresser, A. Pearn, chemist, and the little shop on the end belonged to W.J. Tarr, who was a local builder. (McCarthy)

Staff of H. Mason and Son, undertakers and joiners, seen here in Cecil Road where they had their business, 1932. Their phone number was Lancing 84. The company later combined forces with H. Starkey, a builder in Lancing, and the company became known as Starkey and Mason, funeral directors, trading from South Street. The company was later sold to H.D. Tribes. Staff here are Bob Mason, Jack Mason, Edward Feldwick jnr, Jim Muggeridge and Henry Mason.

Aburnsons, Coach Builders Ltd, Lancing. The company had their workshop in Mash Barn Lane. This photo shows the 'skeleton' stage of construction of a coach; the covering bodywork would have been applied next, and thereafter internal trims and seats added. The coach would then be ready for the road. This photo was taken outside the works.

Some of the staff of Aburnsons. This photo and the previous one of the coach were both taken in about 1946. A few years afterwards the company ceased trading, after about ten years in existence.

A.G. Colbourne's horse and cart making deliveries in The Street at North Lancing, *c.* 1915. After starting up the business Mr Colbourne had a shop built on the corner of Penhill Road and South Street, but while it was being constructed he was killed when he fell from a cart while visiting his firm's branch in Findon. He was only forty-one when he died. Some of his elder sons took over the running of the firm. Mrs Aylmore is the lady at the door of Hawthorn Cottage. (Wells)

W. Weller, builders and smiths, Sompting, June 1927. Weller's premises were at the eastern end of West Street, next to Ball Tree Cottages. Mr Weller is the gentleman in the front with the walking stick and carpenter's rule in his hand. The smith is standing on the far right, clearly identifiable by his leather apron. Mr Homewood, Mr Knight, Mr Ward, Mr Brockhurst, Mr Messer and Mr Jago are some of the other tradesmen.

Pullen-Burry's movable greenhouse, 1913. This was the first year of use for the greenhouse which had watering, heating and ventilating systems combined. Mr Pullen-Burry, on the left in the trilby-style hat, is watching, and perhaps instructing the young lad who is turning a wheel, which in turn is driving the greenhouse, even with all the workers on top. This, I am sure, would have been the maiden voyage! (Edwards)

J. and A. White, general supply stores in West Street, Sompting, *c.* 1913. Mr White is standing in the doorway with his dog, who is looking towards either the pork butcher's section or the cyclist's leg! This shop was later taken over by W. Atterbury & Son, remaining as a general store, but adding a post office and fruiterer's and florist's, which stood where the flint wall is shown on this photo.

Sompting post office, West Street, early twentieth century. It looks like a carefully staged photo with the children all standing quite still, along with the horse and cart. The three boys standing together are outside the post office, the sign of which can be seen on the wall. It was situated in 6 Rooksacre Cottages, adjacent to Trelawney's Cottage.

CHAPTER FOUR

BESIDE THE SEASIDE

Holidaymakers paddling in the sea at South Lancing, 1909. The sort of holiday snap people would take today. Not much has changed really in the way people enjoy their time at the seaside, except for the clothing! All are clearly enjoying the paddle, and the ladies are making sure they don't get their dresses wet. Though the sea is warm enough to go paddling, they are all heavily clothed with coats and hats on.

Edwardian bathing beauties, 1909. Both are in swimwear of the period, covered from the knee upwards, with one woman covering her modesty with her hands. The women were staying in a bungalow called Kingscote on the beach, one of many that made up Bungalow Town. On the back of the postcard one had written: 'we are staying here another week if the weather keeps fine'; clearly they had plenty of time on their hands! (Wintons)

Beach scene at South Lancing, 1906, with the then familiar backdrop of the whitewashed Coastguard cottages. According to the sender of the postcard, the boat in view was quite often on the beach with the owner close at hand, sometimes taking visitors out sailing. This was most probably an additional way of earning money when not fishing. (A.G. Colbourne)

All aboard for the *Skylark*, 1924! The boat was owned by the landlord of the Three Horse Shoes pub, George Prideaux. He is seen here at the stern sitting on the side; his brother Leo is at the bow leaning over the side. They used the boat for taking out day trippers for rides along the coastline. A plug for the pub's brewers, Tamplins, is clear for all to see, pronouncing that these locals were fed on Tamplins' ales and stout!

South Lancing from the seafront looking north, *c.* 1909. The sender of the postcard has clearly marked where she was staying, the convalescent home, Mount Herman. After being at the home for a week she wrote 'my fingers are a little better, but my thumb still has to be poulticed'. The large building to the right is The Chestnuts, another convalescent home. (McCarthy)

The same view as the previous photo, but this time it's after a storm in 1910: the sea has flooded on to the Beach Green, a.k.a. Sea Green. The boats were brought up from the beach, and moored to the 'island' for safe keeping during the storm. The Three Horse Shoes can be seen, with the Tamplins advert on the gable end. Just below the pub, in the backwater, is an old disused goods wagon from the Lancing Carriage Works. (McCarthy)

The charred remains of the bungalow Kittiwake. The bungalow was on the beach at the east end of the Widewater. Mr B.W. Godfrey was living here when it burnt down, in August 1911. As the bungalow was built around two wooden carriages there wasn't much left after the blaze. The cause was most probably a fallen oil lantern, used for lighting at the time. It seems the only parts to survive were made of iron, including the corrugated roof, pots and pans and the bedstead. (F. Rowe)

'Lancing bungalows after the great storm, 16 December 1910', is the rather dramatic title for this postcard, but then any storm would seem like a great storm when your home was situated just above the high water line, as this photo clearly shows. Some of the owners have put up hurdles, a framework of split timber, bonded together by withes to help protect against such storms. They also boarded up the windows and doors to protect the glass. (McCarthy)

Relics of old English battleships. Two figureheads, originally carved for the bows of ships to placate the gods and drive away evil spirits, are seen here in a garden at Bungalow Town. HMS *Pearl* and HMS *Scylla* are the names of the ships. Many of the bungalows had artefacts of a maritime nature, including one that had a mast and rigging in the garden along with two mounted cannon! New Salts Farm and farmhouse at South Lancing are in the background. Lancing College and chapel look resplendent on the hill.

South Lancing beach, *c.* 1959. It looks like a Silver Cross convention, or a Lancing young mothers' club outing! There are at least sixteen prams in view on the pebbles and the sands, including a twin pram with double hoods. Most of these prams would now be classed as collectable! (Wardells)

Mermaid bathing café, early 1940s. Before becoming a café the building was a private house, built in about 1916, called Redcroft. The building still exists, housing a café and amusement arcade, ever popular with tourists and locals. To the eastern end of the building were changing cubicles that you could use for a charge of 1*d*, or you could hire a deckchair for 3*d*.

CHAPTER FIVE

SPORT

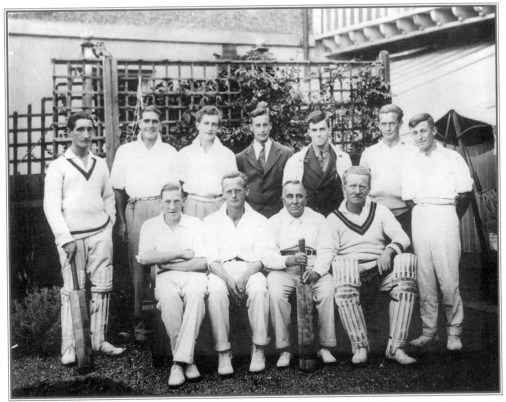

Lancing Excelsior cricket team, c. 1930, in the back garden of Lancia in the Lower Brighton Road, South Lancing, home of Johnnie Neil. The team was the brainchild of Mr Neil and started in about 1920, when he arrived in Lancing. The last game of cricket he played was at Monks Rec in 1939, at the age of seventy-five! Standing, left to right: Len Glover, Alex Page, George Lisher, Mr Collins, Mr Penegue, -?-, Ernie King. Seated: Keith Russell, George Starkey, Johnnie Neil, Mr Crombie.

Members of Lancing Athletic cricket club outside the old pavilion at the manor. The match that was taking place was a friendly, against Sompting, on Christmas Eve in 1950. Lancing Athletic was officially founded in 1942. George Cannons, seen here third from the left at the front, was one of the founder members; he also played football for Lancing Football Club for many years.

During the war years, in 1941, an attempt was made to put together a Lancing ladies' cricket team. The instigator was the well-known Lancing sportsman George Cannons. The team got together for a few practice sessions, but never got to play any matches and disbanded. The team to be was, left to right: Tiny Webster (coach), ? Glazebrook, Madge Perry, ? Murphy, Pamela Pounsett, Dolly Strudwick, Alma Gardener, Molly Strudwick, Lyn Marshall, Mary Sear, Renee Groves, George Cannons (coach).

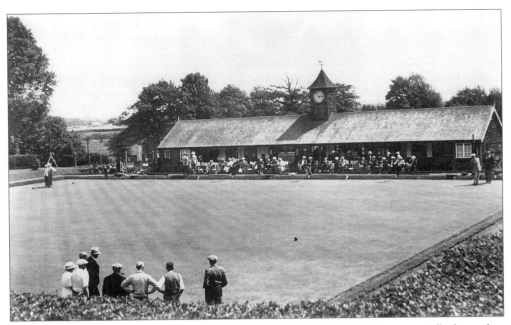

The old cricket pavilion, home to the Lancing bowling club as well as the cricket team. Sadly the pavilion was destroyed by fire in 1975. Members of the bowling club are seen here enjoying a game. The club was founded in 1937, the founder president being C.F. Pycroft, a local nurseryman, who had the pavilion built. Some of the other founder members were Cliff Davies, Fred Picknell, Jack Harber, George Cox, Arthur Chubb, Jack Hildrew, Ken Batten and George Challis. Honours include the Sussex County Secretaries Cup in 1952 and 1967, and the British Legion south-east area (singles) in 1969. Sixty-one years later, and the club is still bowling!

Boys' Brigade camp at Lancing, 1914. A three-legged race is in full swing with plenty of admirers looking on. The boys were more than likely the Boys' Brigade from Brighton, as they quite often frequented both Lancing and Sompting. The number of tents in view confirms that they were a large group. (Wiles)

Three Horse Shoes quoits team, 1907. Standing, left to right: Eli Warr, Harry Fakenbridge, -?-, Charlie Matten, Billy Babb, George Haller, Edwin Fuller, Mart Fuller. Seated: Tom Till, Cephas Gammans, George Humphrey, Charlie Humphrey, Sam Warr. Quoits is not a sport played much now, but in the early 1900s it was popular. The circular ring, made of iron, was thrown at a mark on the ground; a compass, to be seen in front of George Humphrey, was used for measuring distances when it came to seeing who won, and saved any arguing!

Quoits being played on an old brickfield site situated on the south side of Penhill Road, South Lancing, c. 1908. The brickfield was in existence in 1861 and had ceased production by the turn of the century. A secondary railway line ran from the brickfield towards Freshbrook Road, which then joined up with another line from an old gravel pit and then headed west alongside the main line, eventually joining the main line just before the crossing gates. The Beach Green was another site where the quoits team played. The team's headquarters was at this time the Three Horse Shoes pub.

Lancing United FC pictured in the season of 1921/22. Back row, left to right: 'Dodger' Merriott, Joe Smotten, Len Lawrence, Alec Battrick, Henry Steer. Middle row: Bill Scrase, H. Carter, Fred Peters. Front row: Rupert Battrick, 'Buller' Battrick, Gordon Barrett, Ted Edwards, Ted Monnery.

Abbey Rovers FC outside the changing rooms at Croshaw Rec, 1963. Standing, left to right: Tom Brown, -?-, Andy Wood, Dave Elliott, Peter Hugget, John Dixon, Brian Wells, Chris Rovik, Roy Cooper. Kneeling: Paul Aldridge, Tommy Brown, Mick Lewington, Eddie Fry, John Godfrey, Terry Parker, Ernie France.

Sompting Football Club, 1935/36, winners of the Charity Cup, Croshaw Cup and League runners-up.
Standing, left to right: Jack Skinner, Mick Smyth, Mr Coleman, Bob Woolgar, Horace Stovell, -?-.
Kneeling: Mr Francis, -?-, Bill Riddles, Vic Osborne, -?-, Nana Bushby.

Sompting Youth Club, 1945/46, proudly displaying a cup. Standing, left to right: Harry Weller, Les
Firman, Bill Rolf, Eddie Smith, Stan Tilly, 'Nobby' Newman, Bill Brewster. Seated: Phil Green, Dave
Green, Bill Knight, Fred Brockhurst, Reg Marsh.

CHAPTER SIX

IN PERSON

Francis Trevett, seen here in 1880, was the village tailor from 1842 to 1887 at South Lancing.
His workplace was at the north end of Blenheim Terrace (built in about 1842) in South Street. At the
other end of the terrace was Trevett's sweet shop which Francis set up. Colonel Lloyd, lord of the manor,
was one of his customers. In Mr Trevett's work book an entry in 1865 for Colonel Lloyd includes: 'to make
stable suit with wolling cord £2 17s 0d and a livery suit £3 16s 0d'. The tailor's rate for labour
was 3s 6d a day! (W. Page)

Charles jnr and Rose Gammans with their two children, Nora and Hubert, locally known as Cecil, in the garden of their home in South Lancing, c. 1910. Charles Gammans had stables and buildings in Penhill Road where he carried out his business as a carrier, with his horse and cart. Charles' father, Charles snr, was a local brickmaker, sand and beach merchant. Cephas Gammans, another family member, was also a brickmaker, a trade the family were involved in from about 1882 until the 1930s.

Miss Odeon, alias Dina Mason, c. 1934, complete with decorated bicycle and a basket full of magazines that the Odeon would send or give out each month free of charge for promotional purposes. The latest big film being advertised on Dina's bike was A Man with Two Faces. The doorman can also be seen outside the Odeon.

Lancing station staff, 1906. Mr Rutter was stationmaster, and lived in the station house that is built on the end of the station office. The station house was also used as the doctor's waiting room and surgery, not that Lancing had a doctor at this time: a doctor from Shoreham was sent for when he was needed. Even for the small village that Lancing was in 1906 a large station staff was required, as most goods went by rail. As Lancing had a large number of nurseries and market gardens there were always plenty of goods to be loaded on to the trains.

Church fête at North Lancing, *c.* 1927. The Revd Edward Curphey Paton, in the hat, was at St James the Less from 1920 to 1933, the year he retired to live on the Isle of Man. Both he and his wife were very popular with the parishioners. While in Lancing he saw his greatest wish realised, the building of the church at South Lancing, St Michael's and all Angels in South Street, thus making it a separate parish.

Members of the Wood family, Jim, Sidney and Florence and friend, at the front of their home, 15 The Street, *c.* 1929. The family bought nos 15, 16 and 17 in The Street, a terrace of three cement and rendered cottages, at auction when a portion of the Lancing manor estate was sold on 20 July 1922. The terrace was locally known as Post Office Cottages, cottage no. 15 being the post office at North Lancing for many years. The cottages still exist. (McCarthy)

A rare photo, dating from 1907. It is the only photo I have seen of Honeyman's Hole, which is situated opposite Sussex Pad public house to the east of Lancing. There were a few of these water holes in Sussex, some legendary; most were said to be bottomless. Honeyman's Hole was one of these, and it is said a coach and horses fell into it one night, never to be seen again! The men here are the village fire brigade testing their hoses. (E.A.)

If only they had had colour film in 1912! What a sight these apples would have looked. This photo was actually taken on the day of a wedding, which is why the men are all dressed up. They are posing in the garden of Holmecroft, the home of Frank Bushby snr. All these men had market gardens or nurseries, and must have thought it was a good opportunity to pose with some of their produce. Note the different forms and weaves of the baskets, which added to the splendour of this photo. (McCarthy)

A couple of old Sompting families coming together with the marriage of Jim Green and Jessie Kennard, both seen here outside Busticle Cottages, Sompting. Note the bride's fine bouquet.

Ernie Souter snr in his garden, *c.* 1939. Ernie came to Sompting in 1920, when he became a chauffeur to Mr Pullen-Burry, the landowner and market gardener. Ernie married Caroline Merritt who came from Ashington. Together they had four children, one boy, Ern jnr, and three girls, Ivy, Peggy and Sylvia. The old dog and chicken in the photo with Ernie both fed together from the same plate!

Evelyn 'Bobby' Styles at the rear, with Peggy Souter sitting on Captain, 1935. They are posing by a haystack in the rick yard of Street Barn Farm, West Street, Sompting. The farm still exists today and is farmed by the Phillips family.

CHAPTER SEVEN

BEST DAYS OF OUR LIVES

Church of England School, Mill Road, North Lancing, 1915. This group photo was taken in front of the school house. Pupils include Michael Burtenshaw, Albert Johns, Samuel Elliott, Bob Upfield, Georgina Prideaux, Celia Potter, Molly Proctor, Doris Weaver and Eileen Saunders. These photo get-togethers were not very popular with the children, as you can see! One of the main problems was the time they had to sit still, because of the lengthy exposure time of the camera.

Church of England School, 1918. Back row, left to right: Sidney Chatfield, Ernest Colbourne, -?-, Ena Prideaux, -?-, -?-, George Sharp, -?-, Michael Burtenshaw, Albert Johns. Middle row: Olive Lisher, -?-, -?-, Ethel Howard, -?-, -?-, -?-, Eileen Saunders, Kitty Kenward, Nelly Minter, Ivy Hall. Front row: Alex Page, Bob Upfield, Samuel Elliott, Eddy Gregory, Stanley White, -?-, George Kimber. The teachers are Miss Lane and Florrie Heaton.

Lancing Corner, 1906. This is the site of the manor roundabout at North Lancing. The small copse of trees was a popular place for some of the pupils from the village school at North Lancing. At lunchtime they would come here to amuse themselves. I was told of one particular time when a boy decided to give an impromptu biology lesson to the girls who were present, by putting a worm on a house brick and then chopping it up into little pieces! The boy's name shall remain a secret! (Mason)

Even as the years passed by, these school photos still did not seem to be popular with the children. This one was taken in 1936, in the largest room at the C. of E. School. Most of the pupils have a toy with them. You hear complaints about class sizes nowadays, but I wonder how staff would cope with this one; there are at least forty-three pupils.

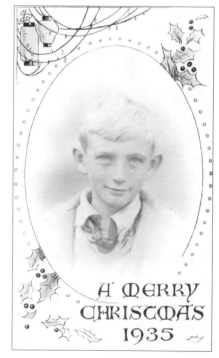

Cyril Fry, born 1928, seen here in 1935 aged seven. Cyril was one of nine children in the family who lived in Church Path, now First Avenue, Lancing. After leaving school Cyril went on to have his own building and builders' merchant business in Crabtree Lane, Lancing.

Brother and sister Jack, a.k.a. Fiddy, and Nancy Mason having their photo taken in the same place as Bessie Upfield in the previous photo, c. 1925. There were four other children in their family. Later in life Jack became the grave digger at Lancing and Sompting cemetery in Upper Boundstone Lane. It was said he would leave half a dozen graves open just in case of an epidemic! Jack, who was well known in the village, dug all the graves by hand.

Bessie Upfield, born in 1915, started her school life in 1924 at North Lancing, where her family were market gardeners. She is posing in the playground. The side of the Old Cottage can be seen behind her.

Lancing Council Infants' School, *c.* 1914. Back row, left to right: -?-, Emily Wood, Raymond Colbourne, -?-, John Mitchell, -?-, Leo Matthews, -?-, 'Joker' Rose, ? Richards, -?-. Middle row: -?-, Michael Burtenshaw, -?-, -?-, May Warr, John Howard, -?-, Gilbert Battrick, Samuel Elliott, Eddy Gregory. Front row: -?-, -?-, -?-, Annie Norris, Alfie Seiver, -?-, Laura Matten, Joan Warr. The teachers are Miss Curd and Miss Trevett. The school was opened in 1914 to help ease the overcrowding at the North Lancing School, caused by an ever increasing population in the village. The school later became known as South Lancing Primary, and it is now called Freshbrook First School.

Teaching staff of South Lancing Primary School in North Road, during the Second World War. All the windows are taped up to prevent them from shattering if there were any near misses from bombs. The teachers here are all female, presumably because the men were fighting for their country. Some of the teachers at the school during the war included Miss Hefford, Miss Cates, Miss Woods and Mrs Birch.

South Lancing Preparatory School, 1925. The school was held in the Wesleyan church buildings, now the Methodist church in South Street. The school was run by Miss McCarthy, whose family were the village photographers. Most of the children who attended were from well-to-do families, the parents being established farmers and nurserymen. Marshall, Phillips, Lisher and Hawkins are names of some of the children here. Miss Bunting ran the school originally, with Miss Perry taking over when Miss McCarthy retired. (McCarthy)

Watching the sports at Lancing College outside the pavilion, 1912. The number of parents on the balcony of the pavilion would suggest it is sports day, a cold and windy one at that! (F. Rowe)

Sompting C. of E. School, c. 1926. Back row, left to right. L. Knight, C. Jenkins, W. Moore, -?-, R. Humphreys, F. Chatfield, A. Bennett, J. Coleman, S. Humphrey, R. Miller, -?-. Middle row: W. Ives, G. Monnery, E. Brown, D. Miller, K. Archard, K. Richardson, -?-, F. Mitchell, E. Souter, J. Harman, W. West. Front row: M. Harman, P. Clapshoe, D. Battrick, E. Evers, C. Scrace, A. Riddles, E. Stovell, E. Lowe, W. Green, E. Richardson. The teacher is Miss Pennicott.

Sompting C. of E. School, Loose Lane, c. 1927. Back row, left to right: George Duffield, Bill Mansfield, John Duffield, Bill Chatfield, -?- (standing slightly in front), Charlie Gatland. Third row: Ern Cuckney, Fred Ounson, Winnie Bashford, Renie Etherington, Jack Beecher, Ern Heather. Second row: Kitty Brockhurst, Verdy Bampton, Gladys Nye, Rose Chatfield, Elsie Stringer, Mable Reason, Ivy Town, Dorothy Hide. Front row: Gilbert Evans, Vic Ives, Sid Simmonds, Fred Trussler, John Archard, Tom West. The photo was taken in the recreation ground.

Although this photo is not in very good condition, I felt it was pictorially interesting and unusual. It shows a cookery class from the school at Sompting. The lesson was taken in the Reading Room by Miss Owen, who travelled around different schools teaching cookery. Back row, left to right: Florrie Homewood, Marjorie Kennard, Nancy Hollis. Middle row: Winnie Bashford, Rosy Chatfield, Gladys Nye, Winnie Kimber, Kath Bennett, Vi Beecher, Daisy Evans, Emily Sandford. Front row: Jessie Simmonds, Ivy Town.

Sompting Primary School, Class 3, 1952. Back row, left to right: -?-, Martin Wakeham, Tony Feldburgh, Richard Paskin, Michael Wakeham, -?-, Rodney Bumbey, Clifford ?, John Pickles, John Moore, ? Souter, -?-. Front row: Alan Rankin, Lesley Cowdrey, Sandra Cox, Mary Jones, Prunella Pennells, Marilyn Dorey, Ann ?, ? Bradley, -?-, -?-.

CHAPTER EIGHT

HIGHWAYS & BYWAYS

Sea Approach, c. 1910. This byway used to meander down from the bottom of South Street to the area of the Mermaid Café. A road now takes roughly the same route, but is more direct. One of William Chorley's convalescent homes, The Chestnuts, can be seen at the top of the Approach. Perhaps the rather grand looking gentleman was in South Lancing convalescing. (McCarthy)

Lancing Park, 1929. This was the first private estate to be built in Lancing; development started in the late 1920s. The two concrete pillars at the entrance still stand today. The sender of this postcard gives an insight into what Lancing was like in the 1920s. 'I have put an X which is the entrance to the carriage works, you ought to see the fields of daffs, they are a picture. Have not been bathing yet, some very pretty walks all around, love from Nelly.' (McCarthy)

Farmers Lane from the east, South Lancing, 1922. Owing to increased development of Kings Road, coming up from the Lower Brighton Road towards Farmers Lane, the inevitable happened: they merged and became one, the whole then being known as Kings Road. The houses, North View, Plasderwen, The Bungalow, whose roof can just be seen behind the hedge, and Hillview Terrace are all still standing. The old Farmers Hotel, built in about 1851, can be seen at the far end of the lane. (Ripley)

Freshbrook Road, South Lancing, mid-1950s. At the beginning of the century this area was known as Salt Lake and there was no thoroughfare. At this time Salt Lake was home to many well-known Lancing families: Strudwick, Burtenshaw, Greet, Lisher, Till and Badcock. The road was made up with tarmac during the 1960s. The name Freshbrook comes from a brook that runs through the area.

Lower West Lane, c. 1928. The pair of semi-detached bungalows at the start of the development were called Sundour and Ventura, and both were owned by members of the Durbridge family. Judging by the number of people in view, the lane was a popular walk between North and South Lancing. (McCarthy)

Pratton Avenue, *c.* 1928. When this photo was taken only seven plots of land in Pratton Avenue had been built on. To the left can be seen an Ellman Brown 'For Sale' sign. This company is still in business as estate agents in Shoreham-by-Sea. (McCarthy)

Hamilton Road, looking north, *c.* 1938. The bungalows in the road were priced between £525 and £625! In the distance on the southern slope of the downs is the ongoing development of the Fircroft Estate, which took its name from Fircroft House that stood in the area.

This view, looking from south to north, is the northern end of Grinstead Lane, Lancing. The lane was named in about 1928: it is thought the name commemorates the fact that the tithes were paid to West Grinstead. (Wells)

Lynchmere Avenue, North Lancing, *c.* 1950. The avenue at this time did not run into Firle Road as it does now, but finished halfway up and continued into Fircroft Avenue. The bungalows of Firle and Derek Road are in view at the top of the hill. Note the unmade road and pavements; the road was made up in about 1962. (Wardells)

Boundstone Lane, 1926. This was the western boundary between Lancing and Sompting, clearly still a lane at the time this photo was taken. The old chap sitting by the wayside looks very much like a 'gentleman of the road'. One such gentleman who used to spend a lot of his time in this area was known as 'Juicy' to the locals, because of his habit of chewing and spitting tobacco!

The old highway that runs through what was the original village at North Lancing: looking west along what is now known as Manor Road, c. 1907. This was a small part of a highway that made its way from Portsmouth to Brighton. The parish church of St James the Less is on the left; parts of the church date back to 1120. The chap with the horse is thought to be Alf Broomfield, who was the village smith at North Lancing, and was often seen leading horses to be shod. The other chap, with the basket on his head, was the fish merchant from South Lancing. (Mezzotint)

Busticle Lane, Sompting, 1930s. This is one of the older highways in the parish, dating back to the eighteenth century. In the 1920s Millfield Cottages, thirty-two in number, were built in Busticle Lane by the council. The area they were built on had previously been used as a prisoner of war camp. Quite noticeable in this photo is the lack of traffic – not so now, as this is one of the busiest roads in Sompting.

West Street, Sompting, c. 1925. Even though this postcard is titled as showing the post office, it doesn't: it actually shows a grocer's shop which belonged to Billy Boxall. It stayed as a grocer's until a few years ago, when it was turned back into a house. The cottage with the children outside was the home of the Heather family. The children were Eddie, Billy and Ernie. The family later moved to 2 Millfield Cottages in Busticle Lane, when their cottage was demolished in the late 1920s. (Ripley)

Latimer Cottages and Edward Terrace, West Street, Sompting. Some well-known Sompting families have lived in these cottages over the years, including Kennard, Riddles, Tugnett and Coleman. The pub sign of the Gardeners Arms shows where it has been since the 1870s, making it the oldest pub in the parish.

Church Lane, Sompting, c. 1935. The lane is aptly named as it leads from the village to the parish church of St Mary's. The six cottages in the lane were called Hermitage Cottages. They were destroyed by a fire in October 1957. The field in the foreground was known locally as 'the park', and was used for the Sussex County and Royal Counties agricultural shows.

CHAPTER NINE

SAY 'CHEESE'

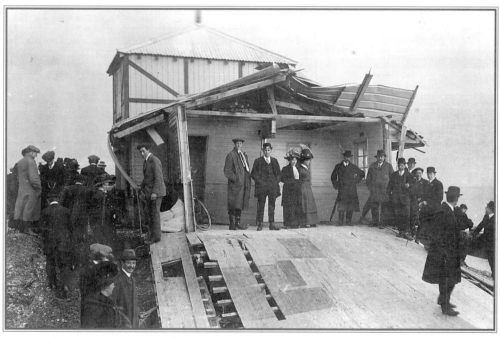

Storm damage to Wild Waves, one of the many bungalows on the beach at South Lancing, making up what was known as Bungalow Town, c. 1912. All the shingle has been washed away from the base of the bungalow making the floor collapse and bringing down the walls as well. When these bungalows were damaged by storms, fire and so on, there would always be a great deal of interest and large crowds. Most of the people here look quite serene and happy, so I wouldn't have thought any of them was the owner!

Lancing Carriage Works fire brigade, 1914. All these men were volunteers, and most of them lived at Bessborough Terrace. All the houses in the terrace had bells that were connected direct to the works for emergency calls to let them know when they were needed. Standing, left to right: Percy Botting, Mr A. Taylor, Jack Warr, Ernest Green, Will Morley, Mr H. Harland, George Young, Matthew Cluer, Mr Meads, Bert Cluer. Seated: Charlie Richardson, Dick Dunn, Arthur Morris, Mr A. Panter (superintendent), Charlie Meads, Bob Dunn, Herbert Mansfield. Mr Meads was the 'runner' of messages.

Edward Feldwick in his back garden in Cecil Road, South Lancing, 1905, with a fine show of chrysanthemums. His son Edward jnr is standing alongside wearing a very familiar 'snake belt', which I am sure many 'young' lads remember; they were worn right into the early 1960s. Also in this photo is Flo Feldwick, whose face can just be seen peering through the flowers at the back in the centre.

Grand opening of the Empire Club, Penhill Road, on Empire Day, 1924. The club was presented to the people of Lancing by a well-to-do gentleman named G.S. Croshaw. Mr Croshaw was a well-liked and respected gentleman in the village, and is remembered by name through roads in the parish, also Croshaw Rec. The huge cracker was full of presents for the children. The first Hon. Secretary was Mr A. Marriott. When the club opened membership was open to all men from eighteen years upwards with fees at 6s per year and 6d per week to visitors!

Christmas dinner for the old 'uns at the Empire Club in 1935, with entertainment by a local band, The Rascals. The club at this time could not have had adequate heating, looking at the number of people sitting at the tables with their hats and coats on. The younger men standing around the tables were most probably the staff who served the meal.

Elizabeth Mason (née Feldwick), with Winnie Mason in the lovely basinette; Edward Feldwick jnr is the young man. They are all posing opposite the family grocer's shop, E. Feldwick, in North Road, in about 1906. Note how smart Edward, a.k.a. Ted, looks in his three-piece suit and watch and chain. All the trees and hedgerows seen here are long gone and have been replaced by shops, one of which is selling this book!

Blackberrying on Lancing Down. This is not such a popular pastime as it used to be, which makes it more rewarding for the people who partake nowadays. My own family and I go blackberrying on the down most years and are rewarded, thanks to my wife, with lovely 'Lancing' blackberry and apple jam and pies, which I am sure the crop here would have become. The people here are all members of the Mason family, bar one. Back row, left to right: Peggy Mason, Winnie Mason, -?-, Bob Mason. Front row: Nancy and Jack Mason.

A street party in Halewick Close, Sompting, to celebrate the Coronation of Queen Elizabeth, 1953. The close had only twelve houses at this time, so one would imagine all the families are represented here. Families known to have lived here at this time are Drew, Scott, Jackaman, Wise, Green, Wemborn, Attrill, Paine, Bishop, Dunning, Whitfield and Denton.

Farmworkers having a lunch break. The men and the threshing machine worked for W. Langmead who owned Lychpole Farm, Dankton Lane, Sompting. Before being called Lychpole, it was Yew Tree Farm, owned by Ernie Wadman. This photo was taken just after the war in about 1946. Left to right: Bill Leggett, Len Huggett, Alec Huggett, Ted Talbot, Jack Chatfield snr, Reg Moore, Jack Chatfield jnr, Brian Lindfield and Basil Stillwell.

Watching May Day celebrations at Sompting Rec, 1956. Spectators include Doris Bailey, Mrs Osborne, Mrs Bishop, Mrs Edwards, Mrs Allen, Brenda Souter, Kevin Bishop and Mrs Rodd. Once the May queen was selected she would go to see Mrs Wadman at Yew Tree farmhouse, which was where the May queen's dress was kept. The farmhouse can be seen in the background.

Schoolchildren at the Sompting C. of E. School, all dressed up for what looks an Empire Day parade, *c.* 1916. A lot of the children are dressed up in different national costumes of the world. The 'policeman' presumably represented England.

CHAPTER TEN

FARMING

Monks farmhouse, Lancing, on the left with associated buildings and land, 1924. The farmhouse is in North Road and is now known as Monks Farm presbytery. All the old farm buildings are now gone, being replaced by housing. Monks Farm cottages, on the right, housed the farmworkers, one of whom was Arthur Sharp, the cowman, who would take the cows to graze in the field in the foreground. Willie Phillips was the farmer at this time. (Ripley)

Harvesting at Monks Farm, 1924. One would have thought the men were glad to rest awhile to pose for the photographer on what looks like a hot summer's day. (Ripley)

A lovely rural view, looking north up North Road, Lancing, *c.* 1910. The barn just behind the head of the gentleman in the foreground was the last farm building of Monks Farm to go, apart from the farmhouse, and a block of flats is now on the site. The field to the side of the hedge on the right is now Addison Square. Note the fine old elm trees on both sides of the road. Two children can be seen by an old tree stump, known locally as 'the pulpit'. One can only imagine what the children would preach about!

Malthouse farmyard and cottage, *c.* 1900. The actual farmhouse is just out of view to the right of the picture. The farm was one of the largest in Lancing, covering approximately 100 acres, including three barns and other outbuildings. The farm dated from around the middle of the eighteenth century, as did the farmhouse. Like a lot of the old buildings and land, it was owned by the Carr-Lloyd dynasty. The cottage was tied for the workers of the farm. Note the fine array of fowl on view.

Warrie Quelch milking cows at Hoe Court Farm, a.k.a. Lancing College Farm, *c.* 1930. Warrie lived in Hoe Court Cottages. The cow shed is still standing exactly where it was, but there is no longer a milking herd. The cows have their names on slate above them; two are Topsy and Tulip!

Pad Farm was adjacent to the east of the Sussex Pad inn and borders the College Farm and the river Adur. The farmer Edward Passmore also had farming interests at Coombes and Applesham. The farmhouse still exists and is sited behind the Sussex Pad on the College road. This postcard shows the end result of a haystack fire that took place on 18 August 1910. Even in the height of the summer, and putting out a fire, all the men seen are still wearing their caps. (Wiles)

Jack Chatfield snr, *c.* 1928, aerating the ground on a grass field by means of harrowing; the field would later be used for grazing animals. This field was part of Church Farm, Sompting. Church Farm has been farmed by the Phillips family for the last hundred years. Farm buildings and St Mary's church are in the background.

Haystack making at Church Farm, *c.* 1936. The hay can be seen here being forked on to an elevator, which was run by a Lister engine. The hay would then be formed, usually by three men, to make the stack. The stack would be topped off with a thatched, ridged or conical top to keep it dry.

Two of Escott Phillips' farm wagons on the Bostal road, Sompting, *c.* 1947. Sompting Abbots is situated behind the trees. The hay being loaded on to the wagons was taken to Church Farm where it was made into haystacks. Prince is the leading horse, with Rodney behind. Frank Chatfield is leading them.

A binder at work at Sompting, 1930s. The binder, seen here being worked by three horses, tied the sheaves and then put them back in the field where the farm hands would bundle them up, to set up in stooks.

Two fine Sussex farm wagons, one fully laden with sheaves, the other still being loaded. Les Styles ('Nobby') and Jack Chatfield are on the wagon. The boys, who were aged twelve, would earn the grand sum of £3 for their work during the six weeks of the summer holidays. This photo was taken during the 1930s.

CHAPTER ELEVEN

THE YOUNG ONES

Doris and Nellie Day on the sands at South Lancing, 1917. This was the year the Day family came to Lancing to live, taking up rooms initially with Mr Cephas Gammans in Cecil Road. The Gammans family played a major role in the life of Doris; she later married Cecil Gammans, whose father Charles was a local carrier and brickmaker who lived in Cecil Road. Both Doris and Nellie were in the Cheerie Chums, a Lancing concert party that performed at the Parish Hall (see p. 92).

Eileen Fuller, looking radiant in her bonnet, sitting on the lap of her father Frank outside Violet Cottage in South Street, 1916. Violet Cottage was the home of Martin Fuller snr, Eileen's grandfather, who was a prominent figure in the village. He owned many nurseries and belonged to numerous societies, also being a member of the Lancing Parish Council. (McCarthy)

Leslie Till in the flat cap and Charlie Matten outside Yew Tree Cottages in South Street, 1923. Both boys were the same age, born in 1916, and were in the same class at school. The Till family lived in Yew Tree Cottages, while Charlie Matten lived in Seaton Terrace, also in South Street.

Winnie and Jack Mason, 1914. This photo was taken in their home in Cecil Road. Winnie was the eldest of six children born to Elizabeth and Henry Mason.

A children's concert in the Wesleyan church hall, South Lancing, being presented by the pupils of the Wesleyan Preparatory School, c. 1926. The photo has come out quite well, taking into account the year it was taken and the conditions, inside with a flashlight. Two of the girls did not know the photo was going to be taken and have got drill tunics on instead of their costumes. (McCarthy)

A gathering of local children, all dressed up in different national costumes, *c.* 1921. The event was most likely an Empire Day parade. The location may well be the gardens of The Chestnuts, one of the Southern Convalescent Homes; the bearded Mr Chorley, proprietor of the home, can be seen peering over the children at the back.

A happy group of friends posing for the camera in the home of my grandparents, Frank and Eveline Fry, *c.* 1956. The occasion is the birthday of their daughter Rita. Back row, left to right: Jackie Patterson, Pamela Barker, Barbara Bartlett, Audrey Mann, Brenda Grover. Middle row: Sylvia Hudd, Rita Fry, Barbara Mann. My sister Lyn (Lynette) Fry is at the front.

Ray and Derek Fry, seen here in 1939, no doubt wondering what to get up to next! The brothers were never short of playmates coming from a family of nine children – five boys and four girls. Their father Frank and their grandfather Albert snr were both in the building industry. Derek, along with three of his brothers, was also involved in the building industry. Ray was the exception and made a career stewarding on the *QE2* cruise liner.

Members of the Stone family outside their home in Orchard Way, *c.* 1935. Mother Jane is holding Lily with elder sister Joan standing in front of the gate. To date, this house has had three different numbers, because of changes in the road as more development has taken place. Here it is no. 32. When it was built it was no. 9.

Hilda and Emily Wood in front of 17 The Street, North Lancing, 1920. Sadly Hilda, in the white dress, died of consumption, otherwise known as TB, at the age of seventeen. Emily is still alive and well and still resides in Lancing. (McCarthy)

Lancing Wesleyan Sunday school outing, 1910. These outings were enjoyed by the children, and they included frequent visits to the beach at South Lancing. Mr Cephas Gammans snr, a local brickmaker, was an active worker on behalf of the Wesleyan Church, founded the Band of Hope in Lancing, and was one of the earliest members and perhaps a founder of the Wesleyan Sunday school, of which he was superintendent for twelve years. There are at least fifty children seen here.

Reg Bushby standing outside his family home, Holmecroft, in Cokeham Lane, Sompting. His family were nurserymen. Holmecroft was built in about 1908.

Members of the Souter family outside their home in Dankton Lane, Sompting, 1924. The boy is Ern jnr, with Peggy sitting on the wall and Ivy next to her. Mum Caroline is at the back. Ern must have eaten plenty of vegetables when he was young, as he went on to have a family of one girl and nine boys!

Win and Percy Bashford outside their home, Balltree Cottage, 1921. The cottage was one of two together, locally known as Bashford's Cottages. Alan Bashford, the children's father, lived in the one seen here, while Tom Bashford, their uncle, lived next door. Both Win and Percy were born in the cottage. The postcard has been made into an occasion card by having 'Hearty Greetings' overprinted in the corner.

Cousins Alan and Geoffrey Osborne with their May Day garlands in the old Sompting Rec, which was behind Loose Lane. The canteen of the National School is the building behind the boundary wall. This photo was taken in about 1946. Geoffrey's dad Vic played football for Sompting for many years.

CHAPTER TWELVE

THE AIRPORT

Situated at the eastern end of the parish in Lancing is Shoreham Airport, at the moment in joint ownership between Brighton, Hove and Worthing councils. The airport is one of the earliest airfields and is also the oldest public licensed airfield in the country. The first flight from the airport was made in 1910 by an entertainer, Hal Piffard, a Lancing College old boy. The airport played its part during both world wars, including direct support of the allied landings at Dieppe, France, in 1942. An important addition to the airport in recent years has been the police and air ambulance helicopter.

Mr Oscar Morison's Blériot monoplane in the grounds of Lancing College, 11 March 1911. The aviator was invited to make a visit to the college to display his monoplane to the pupils. Mr Morison was an early aviator, and before making the airport at Lancing his base he had spent some weeks making demonstration flights at Brighton. In the summer of 1911 he made the first flight from Paris to Shoreham airport, in twelve hours in a new racing monoplane. He also raced other aviators along the coast, which aroused much amusement and interest among local people. (Wilton jnr)

Oscar Morison, it seems, was a well-to-do gentleman with plenty of money. This showed in the various planes he owned and flew. One of his planes, a Bristol Boxkite, pieces of which are seen here in 1911, was probably due to go into the cladded building, known as Piffard's Shed, to be constructed and made ready for flying. (F. Rowe)

Cecil and Eric Pashley, aviators, with their Farman biplane in about 1912 outside the hangars at the airport. The brothers founded the Southern Aero Club in 1913, along with the most successful flying school in Britain. Eric has his hand on his hip, and Cecil is the one wearing the cap leaning on a wing of the plane. Cecil, who died in 1969, has recently had a restored Tiger Moth named in his memory; it is called the Spirit of Pashley. Eric joined the Royal Flying Corps in 1916 and was killed in action over France. (Winton)

Preparing, repairing, anticipating and realising was surely an apt way of explaining these early days of aviation. This postcard was produced in about 1919.

Autogyro G.ABFZ on show at the airport, 1932. The autogyro is like a helicopter, in that it uses a horizontal propeller for vertical ascent and descent.

Founder members of the Shoreham Aero Club, 1935. The club is still going today.

Trans Channel Airways offered a very popular flight in this De Havilland Rapide between the airport and the Channel Islands. After landing at the airport passengers would be obliged to go through customs. As there were no permanent customs officers at the airport, customs officers from Shoreham Port Authority were brought in to deal with them. Reg Wingfield and Ron Searle, who both worked at the airport, are standing by the plane.

A Mew Gull racing plane, c. 1952. Since 1911 the airport has played its part in air races, including the Kings Cup races in the 1930s. The Art Deco-style airport buildings were opened on 13 June 1936. The airport terminal is now a Grade II listed building. The two trucks behind the plane are the resident ambulance and fire tender.

Number 72, a Proctor racing plane, in front of the airport building, *c.* 1952.

An Auster, G-AIGE, on a visit from Southend-on-Sea municipal flying school, preparing to take off, *c.* 1952. The flying clubs at Shoreham Airport, Redhill and Southend would use each other's facilities when flying around the southern area.

CHAPTER THIRTEEN

CARNIVALS & ENTERTAINMENT

The Martians are coming! This Fireball XL5 float was entered by my family in three different carnival processions, Lancing, Worthing and Brighton. At the Brighton event it was given first place. The float took a lot of time and effort and was built mainly by Cyril Fry and a friend, Don Clark. The truck was loaned by C.B. Fry's, the builders' merchants in Crabtree Lane, Lancing. Left to right: Martin Clark, Adrian Cumberworth, Ian Cumberworth, Malcolm Fry, Philip Fry. Standing behind: Ronald Clark, Martin Fry, Christopher Fry (peeping). On the rocket: Paul Fry, Peter Fry. The photo was taken in 1966.

A float in what I believe was a hospital parade, *c.* 1924. These parades collected money for the local hospital and health care in general. The men of the village would also proudly show their allegiance to their chosen friendly society by wearing the appropriate regalia, as seen here. The Loyal Southdown Lodge, Oddfellows and Jacobites were some that were supported in Lancing at this time. Mr Green, Hector Boyd, Peggy Kimber and Joan Prideaux are some of the participants here.

Lancing and Sompting St John's Ambulance Brigade, taking part in a carnival parade, marching past Chesham Terrace by the corner of Roberts Road and South Street, *c.* 1960. As usual with these carnivals, a good crowd lined the streets. This photo was taken by Eric Surfleet, whose shop was on the corner of Roberts Road. (Surfleet)

Lancing Jubilee Bonfire Boys at Lancing Beach Green, *c.* 1927. Like most Sussex villages and towns, Lancing always used to celebrate 'the 5th' with great enthusiasm and gusto. At one time there were 100-plus Boys, who had their headquarters at the Railway Hotel, now the Merry Monk. After parading through the village, the Boys would make their way to a field where a bonfire was lit. When the fire was well alight Guy Fawkes was committed to the flames. Cecil Gammans, Jack Coleman and Tom Boyd are three of the Boys shown here.

Odeon cinema, Penhill Road, 1934. This photo was taken about a year after it was opened by the Rt. Hon. Earl Winterton, who was an MP. In 1936 the name was changed to the Regal, until 1945 when it reverted to the Odeon. The cinema closed in 1952 and is now part of a small business complex, Regal House. The film *Dinner at Eight* is advertised on the bill board; it would have cost the princely sum of 6*d* to watch!

Lancing's Cheerie Chums giving a concert in aid of the local nursing association at the Parish Hall, *c.* 1928. The Cheerie Chums were quite unique, in that they could stage a fine programme of varied items without the involvement of the opposite sex! The arrangement, scenery and costumes were usually the Chums' own handiwork. Left to right: Doris Day (the Lancing one!), Edna Trevett, Nora Trevett, Gladys White, Mary Lisher, Rose Trevett, Olive White, Ellen Perry, Mary Perry and Nellie Day.

Three entrants for an Empire Day parade, 1937. The parades started from the Empire Club in Penhill Road and would parade through the village at South Lancing. On the left is Will Matten, next to him is Nellie Matten and the fine John Bull is Mr Searle, who had a hairdressing shop next to the old fire station in South Street.

Reg Page outside McCarthy's studio in South Street, 1914. Reg belonged to the Wesleyan church Scouts, which at this time was run by Mr Cass. The small feather in the hat was unique to this pack. It looks very much as if Reg is about to go camping, equipped with his staff, water bottle and haversack. (McCarthy)

Mr C.M. Day and his orchestra, in the garden of the Vicarage at North Lancing, entertaining visitors at a church fête, *c.* 1925. As well as playing in his orchestra, Charlie Day was a member of Lancing Parish Council, on which he served for twenty-five years. He was chairman in 1935. He was also a founder member of the Lancing and Sompting British Legion, based in Culver Road. Mr Day is at the back playing the violin. Mr Cyril Heaton, on the piano, was a master at Lancing C. of E. School at North Lancing.

August bank holiday fête at Lees Meadow, *c.* 1921. Mr G.S. Croshaw gave the piece of land known as Lees Meadow for the use of the parishioners of Lancing and Sompting to use. The land is now known as Croshaw Rec. He was a well-to-do gentleman who lived in a grand house, Lancing Point, which was situated on the Lower Brighton Road. (Ripley)

Hospital fête, Croshaw Rec, *c.* 1925. Nancy Fuller and Phyllis Gammans are in the wonderfully decorated pony chaise, fronted by Millicent the pony. The young jockey is Peter Marshall, who is sitting astride 'Millicent's son'. Percy Marshall is in the top hat and tails. Mr Bastable and Harry Trussler are the other two gentlemen.

A carnival procession, 1969. It is coming out of Cokeham Road, Sompting, into Crabtree Lane, then making its way down North Road into South Street and on to Beach Green. The first float here, being towed by the tractor, has the carnival queen and her two attendants in the trailer behind. The three girls would have been selected at the carnival dance, which was held about a month prior to the carnival. Davis' fun fair and a fireworks' display were also part of the carnival celebrations, all fondly remembered and enjoyed by many.

May Day parade in Church Lane, Sompting, 1912. A fully decorated cart is being led by a donkey, with what looks like the May queen inside.

The 1st Sompting Brownie pack inside the Church Hall of the United Reformed church in Cokeham Road, Sompting. This pack was formed in about 1944 by Kate Thorpe, who was Brown Owl, while Irene Barnard was Tawny Owl; both of them can be seen here. The Brownies include Prunella Pennells, Lyn Tuggnet, Lynda Messer, Jenifer Paskin, Marion Higley, Sandra Cox and Sandra Miller.

CHAPTER FOURTEEN

MILITARY MATTERS

Lancing camp, 1915 – a very rare postcard. This photo was taken in front of Bessborough Terrace, part of which can be seen behind the bell tent. These men were from 196 Company, armed service corps. They were also known as the 'fetchers and carriers' for front line troops. It is assumed that Lancing was a training camp for recruits before they were shipped off to France. These were the main guard on the gates of Lancing camp. (McCarthy)

A family portrait, 1917. George Albert Trevett is sitting with his son, Roger, on the left and his son-in-law, John Sear, behind him. After the war Roger stayed in a uniform and joined the Metropolitan police. Before the First World War George Trevett ran the Southdown Bakery, a family concern in Alma Street, South Lancing. The bakery was awarded gold medals at a bakers' exhibition in 1906. The bakery building is now Chanctonbury Laundry.

Indian soldiers, just one part of the colonial forces called to arms to fight for the Empire during the First World War, are seen here outside The Chestnuts convalescent home at the bottom of South Street. The Chestnuts was one of the homes used during the war for the wounded. A military hospital was set up farther along the coast for these Indians in the Brighton Royal Pavilion. (McCarthy)

Billeted soldiers at home with the Gammans family in their garden at Cecil Road, South Lancing, 1915. At the rear are Rose and Charles Gammans, who is holding his daughter Phyllis. In front of the soldiers are Hubert Gammans (Cecil) and his sister Nora.

On parade, 1915! Cecil Gammans aged ten dressed up in one of the soldier's tunics, complete with his cane. This photo clearly shows what a good relationship was forged between the soldiers and the locals, during what must have been a very stressful time in their lives.

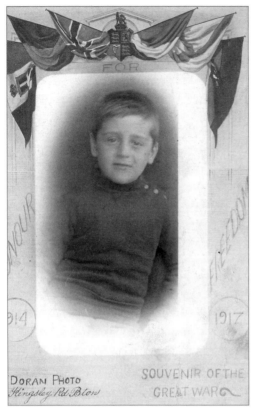

Souvenir of the First World War. This and the following photo were taken to celebrate the end of the war. The young man is George Prideaux jnr. His father was the landlord of the Three Horse Shoes pub in South Street, South Lancing. (F. Doran)

This young lady is Georgina (Ena) Prideaux, sister to George. Both of these photos were taken by F. Doran, a Brighton photographer. He probably travelled around the local villages to take photos like these. One assumes he would have done a good trade, especially as such a major occasion was being celebrated. (F. Doran)

THE OLD SHOREHAM ROAD.
LANCING COLLEGE..O.T.C. ON THE MARCH. No37.

Lancing College officer training corps on a march through Shoreham, along the Old Shoreham Road, with Freehold Street on their left.

One of two Pullmans used during the Second World War by the railway works manager, so he was able to live on site twenty-four hours a day. Because of the important government business being carried out during the war at the works at South Lancing a steam engine was kept in steam at all times coupled to a goods train, which in the event of an imminent landing by the Germans would be loaded up with all vital parts and documents; they would then be transported up country to safety by the works manager or his under manager.

William Chatfield, Sompting-born in 1918, shown here in 1935 in his naval uniform while at training school. William later became a pilot in the Fleet Air Arm. Sadly he was killed at the young age of twenty-two, shot down while flying a plane from his ship, the *Formidable*, off Malta.

Prisoners of war at work during the Second World War. The field they are working in is adjacent to Stocks House (now flats) and Peter Phillips' farm in West Street. I am told that the local kids from both villages would do their bit for the war effort by using the POWs as target practice for their catapults!

Peter Pescod, Lancing-born in 1916. This photo shows him in 1938 at the age of twenty-two. Peter served in the Royal Navy as a stoker on the battleship *Barham*, which was torpedoed by a U-boat around Christmas time, 1939, while in the Arctic. Peter and his ship survived. The *Barham* was later blown up while in the Mediterranean with the loss of about 835 men. I am glad to say that Peter survived and now resides in Sompting.

An area of Beach Green at South Lancing, just after the Second World War in 1946, covered in military defence obstacles. Tenders were invited for the clearance of the obstacles from about 600 yd of the foreshore in December 1945. The acceptance of such a tender was subject to the approval of the War Department. The clearance never happened and the blocks were left and covered over with dirt, and later grass. This formed the landscape that is so familiar today. A bulldozer can be seen on top of the blocks shifting the dirt.

CHAPTER FIFTEEN

McCarthy Brothers

South Lancing beach, 1912. A nice relaxed photo of members of the McCarthy and Austen families. Connie McCarthy, née Austen, became the wife of Eric, who is absent from this photo, most probably behind the camera. Left to right: Dorothy Austen, Mary McCarthy, William McCarthy, Florence Austen, -?-, -?-, Connie McCarthy, Faith Austen, Eileen McCarthy, -?-, -?-. Norman McCarthy is lying at the front. Bessborough Terrace and the Coastguard Cottages are in the background. (McCarthy)

Another group photo of members of the family on the beach, *c.* 1910. This looks very much like time for the children, two of whom are chasing each other at the rear – kiss chase perhaps! Note the way they have covered part of the breakwater up with a cloth, which the boy on the left is leaning against; this was probably to stop being scratched by the barnacles and mussels that would have adorned it. (McCarthy)

Ada Cottage, Salt Lake (now Freshbrook) Road, South Lancing, c. 1909. Eric McCarthy can be seen here admiring the flowers under the canopy. Gladys McCarthy, his sister, is standing, posing for the camera, something I am sure she was quite used to. The McCarthy family may have been visiting Mr Page who lived at Ada Cottage at the time. (McCarthy)

Gladys McCarthy, 1915. Gladys was a member of a local troupe at Worthing known as C. Adolf Seebold's Worthing Whimsies, which was eight people who performed at Mr Seebold's Kursaal on Worthing seafront. (McCarthy)

The wedding of Gladys McCarthy to Phil Gosselin, 1925. This photo was taken in the garden at the Old Tithe Barn. Gladys and Phil are sitting in front of the table. (McCarthy)

The wedding of Norman McCarthy to Violet Grieves, 1932. The photo was taken in front of the Old Tithe Barn, North Lancing. Around this time Norman was the proprietor of Fircroft House, running it as a guest house. Norman died in 1945, and his wife Violet continued to run the guest house for some years afterwards. (McCarthy)

Eric McCarthy was not only a superb
photographer, but also a talented musician.
Here he is with his violin against a theatrical
backdrop. This photo was taken in about 1920.
(McCarthy)

Eric once again showing off his musical talent, playing the banjo, next to the piano player. The band was
known as the New Blackbird Dance Orchestra. This photo was taken in 1928. (McCarthy)

Eric, born in 1890, is seen here in about 1910, among the stooks in a field just to the west of Mill Road, North Lancing. During the 1920s Norman, his brother, gave up photography, but Eric carried on taking photos until his untimely death in 1931, of dental sepsis, aged forty-one. (McCarthy)

CHAPTER SIXTEEN

ROOF OVER OUR HEADS

Beach house, 1910. This is one of the many bungalows that were situated on the beach between South Lancing and Shoreham-by-Sea. The small compartment on the side is the toilet, also known as 'the sentry box'. The trap at the top was for fresh air! There was no main drainage at this time, so the toilets had to be emptied manually. A special bucket was used, so when full it could be drawn out through the trap at the bottom that can be seen here. This job was done every other day by two men in a vehicle appropriately called the lavender cart! (McCarthy)

Orange Girl and Rendez Vous, two elegant houses in the Lower Brighton Road, South Lancing. Both were built in about 1929 and were of quite individual character. The road was starting to get quite heavily developed by this time and a sign advertises 'a valuable building plot for sale' by Chandlers, who were auctioneers and estate agents based in the road. Both houses still exist today. (McCarthy)

Nanette and Boleyn, c. 1929. These two houses were built in 1929 on the south side of the Lower Brighton Road. To the right of the garage was a private beach with private bathing beach tents. Both the houses still exist today. (McCarthy)

Violet Cottage, 1912. This was the home of Martin Fuller snr, local nurseryman and market gardener. It stood on the corner of South Street and the entrance to Elm Grove. This lovely cottage somehow had a fairy tale look about it! As one would expect from a nurseryman, the garden was beautiful. In 1911 Violet Cottage became known as Coronation Cottage for a short time, having been planted out in red, white and blue shrubs and plants in celebration of King George V's Coronation. Martin and Martin Fuller jnr are standing outside the front door. Sadly the cottage was demolished in about 1961. (McCarthy)

Myrtle Cottages, *c.* 1930. This pair of thatched cottages was over the road to the west of the Farmers Hotel. Mr Charles Mason bought two earlier cottages, which were of a flint construction under a tiled roof, and built the pair we see here in 1926. In 1972 they were pulled down and replaced by a row of shops, Farmers Parade. Mrs Green, whose family lived here for many years, can be seen at the window. (Photochrom)

The old Lancing Tabernacle Hall in North Road, just to the north of the railway crossing, in 1927, not long after it was built. Before this meetings had been held in a house in the Lower Brighton Road. Before long the people had outgrown this hall and moved to a new, larger brick-built 'Tab', as it is known locally; this is next to the police station in North Road and opened in 1937. Note the lovely old lamp post. (McCarthy)

These railway cottages were just south of the railway crossing, and were built at around the same time as the extension to the main station house in 1893. The cottages were for staff who worked at the station. They were demolished, I think, in the early 1970s. This photo was taken in about 1965.

Tickencote, the home of Charles F. Pycroft, 1912. When this photo was taken, Tickencote was in Station Road, which is now Sompting Road, Lancing. Charles Pycroft was a fruit grower who owned Belvedere Nursery, also in Station Road. He was also on the Lancing Parish Council. The other house in view is St George's Hall. Both houses are now gone, replaced by flats.

Greenways, a dormer bungalow built in about 1924, in Sompting Road, seen here in about 1928. The glasshouses that can be seen at the back were part of Belvedere Nurseries. These were owned at this time by fruit growers Henery and Grinyer. One assumes that they had bought the nursery of C.F. Pycroft mentioned in the previous caption. Note the young girl with her Jack Russell posing for the camera behind the gate. (McCarthy)

Friars Acre, 1801. The house in Manor Road at North Lancing is brick built and timber framed, and dates to 1659. It has also been known as Newmans Farmhouse and Red Oak Manor. During my schooldays at North Lancing Primary a fellow pupil lived at Friars Acre, and he let it be known that there was a secret passageway between the house and the church, St James the Less, that is adjacent to it!

Cokeham Manor, Cokeham Lane, 1930s. The gardens of the manor were famous in times past for their walnut and fig trees. From 1922 the manor was owned by the Sparkes family, who acquired it from Lord Leconfield. During the war it was occupied by the Army. It was demolished during the 1950s, the land being developed for housing.

Ball Tree Cottages, Sompting, 1916. Members of the Bashford family lived here. They were market gardeners who had land in what is now the Lancing and Sompting cemetery. Note the ball tree in the foreground, hence the name of the cottages. Both these cottages have long since gone.

Busticle Cottages, Busticle Lane, Sompting, *c.* 1936. The cottages were just north of the Ball Tree pub and ran east to west from the side of the road. They were demolished in about 1960 to be replaced by a small industrial estate. L. Knight, H. Ogilvie, A. Kimber, C. Goldsmith and C. Kennard were residents when the photo was taken.

Orchard Cottages, Loose Lane, Sompting, *c.* 1937. This was a terrace of agricultural cottages that were tied for the farm workers. Six of them belonged to Ernie Wadman, farmer at Yew Tree Farm and the other six belonged to Escott Phillips, who farmed at Church Farm. Water was supplied to the homes by wells at either end of the terrace. This water was used for bathing and washing, while drinking water was supplied via a pump that was in the front garden of no. 7. The cottages were demolished in about 1965.

Sunnycroft, West Street, Sompting, in the process of being demolished in 1968. Sunnycroft was owned by L.J. Johnson who was a nurseryman; his nursery was on land west of Church Lane. The name Sunnycroft lives on with a bungalow, which was built in the garden of the original. A gable end of the new bungalow can be seen to the left of the RAC sign that is hanging from The Olde Sussex Tea and Guest House.

Danton Cottages, a.k.a. Dankton Cottages, Sompting, c. 1935. Jack Beacher, who was a shepherd for farmer Ernie Wadman, lived in one cottage; the Pelling family lived in the other.

CHAPTER SEVENTEEN

APPLESHAM & COOMBES

Cuckoo's Corner, on the road to Applesham and Coombes, 1910. This view is much the same today. Still known as Cuckoo's Corner, it has become a popular area for sailing, fishing and walking, with the river Adur close by. (Winton)

The hamlet of Coombes, situated about 1 mile north of Lancing College. Like Lancing and Sompting, Coombes was mentioned in the Domesday Book of 1086. In 1933 West Sussex County Council wanted to change certain boundaries in the county to unite parishes; one of these changes was to unite Lancing and Coombes to come under the combined parish of Lancing. The idea was never implemented; even so Coombes is still associated with North Lancing.

Coombes church, its dedication unknown, sits to the north-east of the parish. It dates from the eleventh century and, like most churches, through the centuries parts of it have been enlarged and altered. Wall paintings were discovered in 1949, and uncovered and treated. The paintings date from c. 1130 to 1753 and consist of symbols and figures. The rectory of Coombes was a separate living until the death of the Revd Edwin Foreman in 1908. It was then joined to North Lancing, which it still is today. (A.H. Fry)

All the parishioners of Coombes celebrated the Coronation of Georve VI in 1937. This photo was taken alongside the Parish Room that was built with money raised by subscription in about 1935. It was at Sheepwash Corner, at the north end of Pump brook, about halfway between Applesham and Coombes.

The Passmore family in the garden at Applesham Farm, 1910. William Passmore started out as a tenant farmer at Coombes in 1901; his family came from the West Country. Eventually he bought the farm and associated lands from Lord Leconfield. The family are still farming today. Standing, left to right: John Wallace Passmore, Arthur Shapland Passmore, Joe Jutsum Passmore, William Dee Passmore. Seated: William Jutsum Passmore, Daisy Edith Passmore, Jane Passmore.

Farm staff at Applesham Farm, 1917. Workers include William Puckett, Harry Peacock, Jack Grumbrell, Freddy Wells, Jim Wittle, Jack Trussler, Alfie Young, 'Me' Pike, Dick Funnel, Obe Everest, Mr Strudwick and Mr Trussler, who was the wheelwright and carpenter. Note that only one gentleman is not wearing a hat or cap!

Dairy Cottage at Applesham, 1910. The farm pond is in the foreground, for use by the horses and cattle. The cottage and pond are both still here today.

Sussex wagon, loaded with wool and waiting to be delivered to the Barnham wool sale, 1910. The auctioneer's name, Stride & Sons of Chichester, is on the bags of wool. William Dee Passmore is the young man wearing the cap.

Mowing grass, west of Coombe Head trees in the west end of Winding Bottom valley, near the great Furze Barn and yard (now gone), c. 1912.

Findon great fair, 14 September 1927. Passmore's won first prize for the best pen of fifty wether lambs. Harry Peacock is on the left, William Puckett is in the flat cap and Fred Woolger is the shepherd in the white coat. Fred had recently arrived to work at Applesham from Saddlescombe. The Robinson family, for whom he had worked, gave up farming in 1926, after seventy-three years.

Ladies' ploughing match, c. 1913. The idea was to see which lady could plough the straightest furrow. This was all part of a fête, organised to raise money for the Wesleyan churches within the Worthing circuit. The event took place on the Downs near Hill Barn at Applesham. W.J. Passmore is the gentleman on the horse on the far right, and looks as if he is about to start the match.

BRITAIN IN OLD PHOTOGRAPHS

SUTTON'S PHOTOGRAPHIC HISTORY OF TRANSPORT

To order any of these titles please telephone our distributor, Littlehampton Book Services on 01903 828800
For a catalogue of these and our other titles please ring Emma Leitch on 01453 731114